Easy Melon Cookbook

50 Delicious Melon Recipes for Drinks, Smoothies, Salsas, Desserts and Soups

By
BookSumo Press
All rights reserved

Published by
http://www.booksumo.com

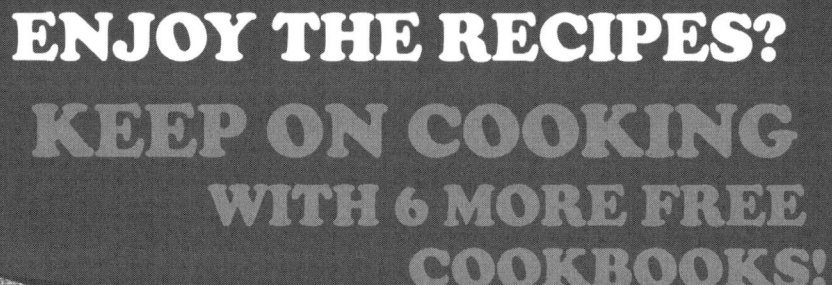

ENJOY THE RECIPES?

KEEP ON COOKING WITH 6 MORE FREE COOKBOOKS!

Visit our website and simply enter your email address to join the club and receive your 6 cookbooks.

http://booksumo.com/magnet

https://www.instagram.com/booksumopress/

https://www.facebook.com/booksumo/

LEGAL NOTES

All Rights Reserved. No Part Of This Book May Be Reproduced Or Transmitted In Any Form Or By Any Means. Photocopying, Posting Online, And / Or Digital Copying Is Strictly Prohibited Unless Written Permission Is Granted By The Book's Publishing Company. Limited Use Of The Book's Text Is Permitted For Use In Reviews Written For The Public.

Table of Contents

Verde Gazpacho 7

Watermelon and Pepper Stir-Fry 8

Lime and Cantaloupe Smoothie 9

Chilled Melon Treat 10

Florida Cooler 11

Summer BBQ Salad 12

South American Inspired Salsa 13

Colorful Appetizer 14

Cream Cheese Melon Tart 15

Seattle Spritzer 16

Casaba Soup 17

Cantaloupe Candy 18

Honeydew Banana Smoothie 19

Watermelon Freezies 20

Traditional Mexican City Juice 21

Bacon Wrapped Snacks 22

Sherbet 101 23

Spicy Fruit Salsa 24

October's Melon Soup 25

Jubilant Juice 26

Picnic Salad 27

Aqua Fresh 28

New Age Pickles 29

Simple Watermelon Salad 31

Best Pool-Side Treat 32

Watermelon Rind Lemongrass Jelly 33

Watermelon Spritzer 34

Traditional Melon Dumplings 35

Watermelon Lunch Box Snack 36

Winter Mint Cocktail 37

3-Ingredient Smoothie 38

Cute Cookies 39

East Latin Chili Lime Melon Snack 41

Simply Watermelon 42

Melon Jell-O Pie 43

Sugar Free Cocktail 44

Maine Inspired Lemonade 45

Red White and Preserves 46

Puppy Dog Slush Pops 47

Country Smoothie 48

Fruit Gazpacho 49

August's Orange Vanilla Smoothie 50

Mexican Melon Juice 51

Southern Rosemary Lemonade 52

Fiesta Candy 53

Party Punch 55

Melon and Cheese Snacks 56

Honey Popsicles 57

Summer Fruit Salad 58

Persian Melon Salad 59

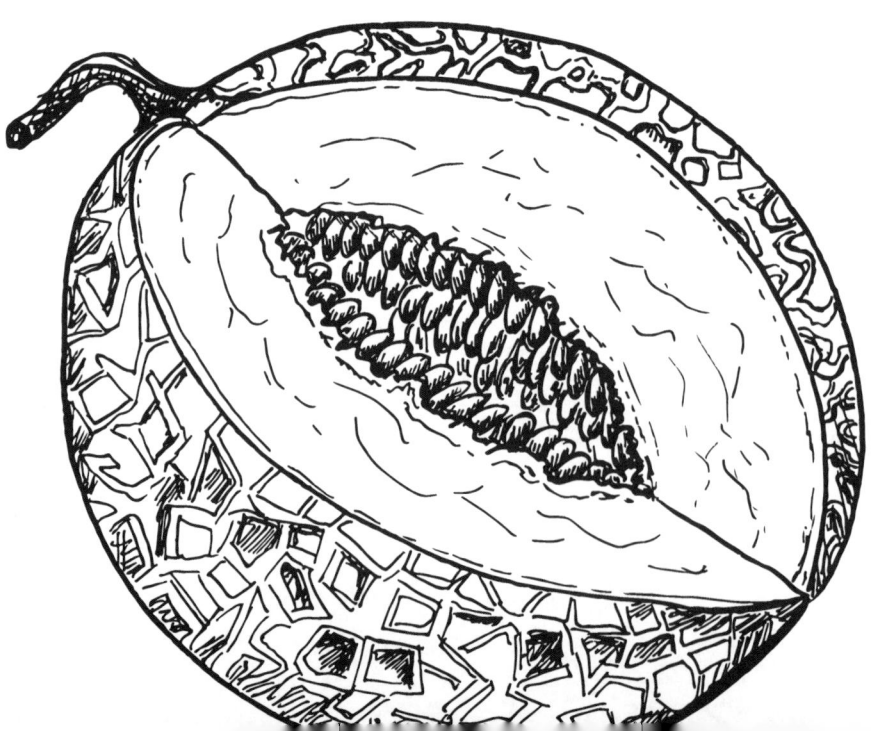

Verde Gazpacho

Prep Time: 25 mins
Total Time: 55 mins

Servings per Recipe: 2
Calories	276 kcal
Fat	15.1 g
Carbohydrates	36.3g
Protein	5.1 g
Cholesterol	0 mg
Sodium	47 mg

Ingredients

- 2 C. diced honeydew melon
- 1 English (seedless) cucumber, peeled and diced
- 1 small onion, diced
- 1 avocado - peeled, pitted, and chopped
- 1 jalapeno pepper, seeded and coarsely chopped
- 1 clove garlic, chopped
- 1/4 C. white balsamic vinegar
- 1 tbsp lime juice
- salt and freshly ground black pepper to taste

Directions

1. Add the following to the bowl of a food processor and puree the mix: black pepper, honeydew, salt, cucumber, lime juice, onion, balsamic vinegar, avocado, garlic, and jalapeno.
2. Puree the mix until it is smooth then add in some pepper and salt.
3. Enjoy.

WATERMELON and Pepper Stir-Fry

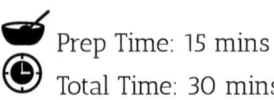

Prep Time: 15 mins
Total Time: 30 mins

Servings per Recipe: 4
Calories   116 kcal
Fat   3.8 g
Carbohydrates   18.3g
Protein   2.6 g
Cholesterol   0 mg
Sodium   1391 mg

Ingredients

- 1 tbsp peanut oil
- 1 onion, thinly sliced
- 3 cloves garlic, minced
- 1 tsp salt
- 1 C. peeled and sliced watermelon rind
- 1 red bell pepper, sliced thin
- 1 C. vegetable broth, divided
- 1/4 C. teriyaki sauce
- 2 tbsps cornstarch

Directions

1. Begin to stir fry your salt, garlic, and onion in peanut oil for 3 mins then add half of the veggie broth, bell peppers, and the watermelon rinds.
2. Now set the heat to low and let the contents cook for 7 mins.
3. Get a bowl, combine: cornstarch, teriyaki, and veggie broth.
4. Add this mix with the onion mix and continue heating everything until it all begins to thicken. Enjoy.

Lime and Cantaloupe Smoothie

Prep Time: 5 mins
Total Time: 5 mins

Servings per Recipe: 4
Calories   70 kcal
Fat   0.2 g
Carbohydrates   18.1g
Protein   0.8 g
Cholesterol   0 mg
Sodium   20 mg

Ingredients

1/4 cantaloupe - peeled, seeded and cubed
1/4 honeydew melon - peeled, seeded and cubed
1 lime, juiced
2 tbsp sugar

Directions

1. In a blender, add the cantaloupe, honeydew, lime juice and sugar and pulse till smooth.
2. Transfer into the glasses and serve.

CHILLED
Melon Treat

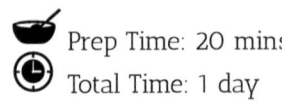

Prep Time: 20 mins
Total Time: 1 day

Servings per Recipe: 6
Calories	123 kcal
Fat	0.6 g
Carbohydrates	30.5g
Protein	2.3 g
Cholesterol	0 mg
Sodium	70 mg

Ingredients

1 large ripe cantaloupe
2 quarts cold water
1 large honeydew melon

Directions

1. Grate the cantaloupe and transfer in a 2 quart pitcher.
2. Fill the pitcher with the water and refrigerate for overnight.
3. With a balling spoon, make little balls from the flesh of the honeydew melon.
4. Add the honeydew melon balls into the cantaloupe mixture just before serving.

Florida Cooler

Prep Time: 10 mins
Total Time: 40 mins

Servings per Recipe: 4
Calories 156 kcal
Fat 1.4 g
Carbohydrates 37g
Protein 1.8 g
Cholesterol 3 mg
Sodium 62 mg

Ingredients

4 1/2 C. cubed honeydew melon
1 1/2 C. lime sherbet
2 tbsp lime juice

4 fresh strawberries (optional)

Directions

1. In a baking sheet, place the honeydew melon in a single layer and freeze, covered for about 30 minutes.
2. In a food processor, transfer the frozen melon with the sherbet and lime juice and pulse till smooth.
3. Transfer the mixture into 4 glasses evenly and serve with a garnishing of the strawberry.
4. Serve immediately.

SUMMER
BBQ Salad

Prep Time: 20 mins
Total Time: 20 mins

Servings per Recipe: 6
Calories   100 kcal
Fat   0.4 g
Carbohydrates   22.7g
Protein   3.3 g
Cholesterol   1 mg
Sodium   39 mg

Ingredients

1 C. lemon yogurt
1 tbsp honey
1 tsp lemon juice
2 C. watermelon balls

2 C. cantaloupe balls
2 C. halved fresh strawberries

Directions

1. In a salad bowl, add the lemon yogurt, honey and lemon juice and beat till smooth.
2. Gently fold in the watermelon balls, cantaloupe balls and strawberries.
3. Serve immediately.

South American Inspired Salsa

Prep Time: 30 mins
Total Time: 2 hrs 30 mins

Servings per Recipe: 14
Calories   32 kcal
Fat   1.1 g
Carbohydrates   5.6 g
Protein   0.8 g
Cholesterol   0 mg
Sodium   9 mg

Ingredients

- 2 large English (hothouse style) cucumbers, finely diced
- 3 C. finely diced fresh cantaloupe
- 1 tbsp extra-virgin olive oil
- 1/2 jalapeno pepper, seeded and minced
- 1 lime, juiced and zested
- 1 small red onion, chopped
- 1 roma (plum) tomato, chopped
- 1 bunch cilantro, coarsely chopped
- 1 pinch salt
- 1 pinch ground black pepper

Directions

1. In a large bowl, mix together the cucumbers, cantaloupe, olive oil, jalapeño pepper, lime juice, lime zest, red onion, tomato, cilantro, salt, and pepper.
2. With a plastic wrap, cover the bowl and refrigerate to chill for at least 2 hours.

COLORFUL
Appetizer

Prep Time: 10 mins
Total Time: 10 mins

Servings per Recipe: 8
Calories   107 kcal
Fat   4.9 g
Carbohydrates   13g
Protein   4 g
Cholesterol   13 mg
Sodium   301 mg

Ingredients

8 cantaloupe balls
8 slices prosciutto
8 green grapes
8 red grapes

8 bamboo toothpicks

Directions

1. Thread a cantaloupe ball, prosciutto slice, green grape, and red grape onto each toothpick and serve.

Cream Cheese Melon Tart

Prep Time: 30 mins
Total Time: 3 hrs

Servings per Recipe: 8
Calories   437 kcal
Fat   25.6 g
Carbohydrates   47.2g
Protein   8.1 g
Cholesterol   52 mg
Sodium   255 mg

Ingredients

- 1/2 (11 oz.) package pie crust mix
- 1 C. sour cream
- 1 egg
- 1 C. ground blanched almonds
- 1/2 C. light corn syrup
- 1/4 tsp almond extract
- 1/2 C. soft style cream cheese with pineapple
- 1 cantaloupe, peeled and seeded
- 1/2 mango, peeled and seeded
- 1/4 C. apple jelly

Directions

1. Set your oven to 375 degrees F before doing anything else and grease a 10-inch round tart pan with a removable bottom.
2. In a small bowl add the pie crust mix and 1/4 C. of the sour cream and stir till moistened.
3. Place the dough onto a generously floured surface and knead for about 12 times.
4. Place the dough in the bottom and up the sides of the prepared pan and press slightly.
5. In another bowl add the egg and beat slightly.
6. Stir in the almonds, corn syrup and almond extract.
7. Transfer the mixture into tart shell evenly.
8. Cook in the oven for about 25-30 minutes.
9. Remove from the oven and cool in pan on a wire rack.
10. In a small bowl, mix together remaining 3/4 C. of the sour cream and cream cheese.
11. Spread the cream cheese mixture over the almond mixture.
12. With a vegetable peeler, slice the peeled melon and mango thinly.
13. Arrange the fruit slices over the filling and refrigerate, covered to chill for up to 2 hours.
14. Before serving in a small pan, melt the apple jelly on medium heat.
15. Coat the melted jelly onto melon and mango and cut into wedges.
16. Serve immediately.

SEATTLE
Spritzer

Prep Time: 15 mins
Total Time: 1 hr 15 mins

Servings per Recipe: 6
Calories 37 kcal
Fat 0.1 g
Carbohydrates 8.3g
Protein 0.7 g
Cholesterol 0 mg
Sodium 72 mg

Ingredients

1 C. cubed honeydew melon
1 C. cubed cantaloupe
1 C. cubed Crenshaw melon
1/4 C. dry lemon lime soda
2 tbsp chopped fresh mint leaves
1 sprig mint leaves, for garnish

Directions

1. In a bowl, add the honeydew melon, cantaloupe, Crenshaw melon cubes, soda and 2 tbsp of the mint and toss to coat.
2. Refrigerate for about 1 hour.
3. Divide into decorative glasses and serve with a garnishing of the mint leaves.

Casaba Soup

Prep Time: 15 mins
Total Time: 15 mins

Servings per Recipe: 4
Calories   134 kcal
Fat   9.2 g
Carbohydrates 13.6 g
Protein   2.5 g
Cholesterol   0 mg
Sodium   123 mg

Ingredients

- 4 C. casaba melon, seeded and cubed
- 3/4 C. coconut milk
- 2 lime juice
- 1 tbsp freshly grated ginger
- 1 pinch salt

Directions

1. In a food processor, add the casaba melon, coconut milk, lime juice, ginger and salt and pulse till smooth.

CANTALOUPE
Candy

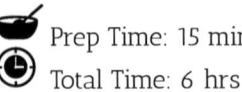
Prep Time: 15 mins
Total Time: 6 hrs 25 mins

Servings per Recipe: 20
Calories	105 kcal
Fat	1.6 g
Carbohydrates	21.8g
Protein	2 g
Cholesterol	5 mg
Sodium	37 mg

Ingredients

4 lb. cantaloupe, shredded
1 (12 fluid oz.) can evaporated milk
2 quarts water

1 1/4 C. white sugar

Directions

1. In a large pitcher, add the cantaloupe, evaporated milk, water and sugar and stir till well combined.
2. Refrigerate for about 10 minutes.
3. Divide the shredded cantaloupe and liquid into the molds and freeze for about 6 hours.

Honeydew Banana Smoothie

Prep Time: 10 mins
Total Time: 10 mins

Servings per Recipe: 2
Calories   254 kcal
Fat   2.8 g
Carbohydrates   57.2g
Protein   5.7 g
Cholesterol   0 mg
Sodium   122 mg

Ingredients

- 1 banana, chopped
- 1/2 honeydew melon, cubed
- 1/2 C. frozen blackberries
- 3 tbsp wheat germ
- 3/4 C. almond milk
- 6 ice cubes

Directions

1. In a blender, add the banana, honeydew melon, blackberries, wheat germ and almond milk and pulse till smooth.
2. Divide ice cubes in 2 tall glasses and place the smoothie over the ice and serve.

WATERMELON
Freezies

Prep Time: 10 mins
Total Time: 10 mins

Servings per Recipe: 4
Calories	110 kcal
Fat	1 g
Carbohydrates	25.1g
Protein	2.2 g
Cholesterol	0 mg
Sodium	46 mg

Ingredients

2 C. cubed cantaloupe
1 1/2 C. ice cubes
1 C. red grapes
1 C. rice milk

6 large mint leaves
4 small cantaloupe wedges

Directions

1. In a blender, add the cantaloupe, ice cubes, grapes, rice milk, and mint leaves and pulse till smooth.
2. Transfer the mixture into the martini glasses and serve with a garnishing of the cantaloupe wedges.

Traditional Mexican City Juice

Prep Time: 10 mins
Total Time: 10 mins

Servings per Recipe: 6
Calories   241 kcal
Fat   5.9 g
Carbohydrates   43g
Protein   5.9 g
Cholesterol   22 mg
Sodium   108 mg

Ingredients

1 cantaloupe, cut into cubes
1 (14 oz.) can sweetened condensed milk
6 C. water
3 C. ice cubes, for serving

Directions

1. In a blender, add the cantaloupe, sweetened condensed milk and water and pulse till smooth.
2. Serve in the tall glasses over the ice.

BACON WRAPPED
Snacks

Prep Time: 25 mins
Total Time: 25 mins

Servings per Recipe: 12
Calories   121 kcal
Fat   6.9 g
Carbohydrates   10.6g
Protein   5 g
Cholesterol   19 mg
Sodium   431 mg

Ingredients

1/4 C. lime juice
1 honeydew melon, fruit removed with a melon baller
9 oz. thinly sliced turkey bacon
36 sprigs fresh mint

Directions

1. In a bowl, place the melon balls and lime juice and gently, stir to coat.
2. With a turkey bacon slice, wrap each ball and secure with a sprig of mint.
3. Arrange on a serving platter and refrigerate before serving.

Sherbet 101

Prep Time: 15 mins
Total Time: 4 hrs 50 mins

Servings per Recipe: 8
Calories	227 kcal
Fat	11.1 g
Carbohydrates	32.1g
Protein	1.8 g
Cholesterol	41 mg
Sodium	63 mg

Ingredients

- 4 C. diced seedless watermelon
- 1 C. white sugar
- 3 tbsp lemon juice
- 1 dash salt
- 1/4 C. cold water
- 1 (.25 oz.) envelope unflavored gelatin
- 1 C. chilled heavy cream

Directions

1. In a large bowl, add the watermelon, sugar, lemon juice and salt and stir to coat evenly.
2. With a plastic wrap, cover the bowl and refrigerate for about 30 minutes.
3. In a blender, add the watermelon mixture and pulse till smooth.
4. Return the mixture into the bowl.
5. In a pan, add the cold water and sprinkle the gelatin over it, then keep aside for about 1 minute.
6. Place the pan on low heat and simmer for about 2 minutes.
7. Add the gelatin mixture into the bowl of the watermelon mixture and stir to combine.
8. Add the heavy cream and with an electric mixer, beat at medium till fluffy.
9. Transfer the mixture into an ice cream maker and freeze according to manufacturer's directions.
10. Transfer ice cream to a lidded plastic container.
11. With a plastic wrap, cover the surface and seal.
12. Freezer for at least 2 hours or overnight.

SPICY Fruit Salsa

Prep Time: 20 mins
Total Time: 1 hr 20 mins

Servings per Recipe: 16
Calories   8 kcal
Fat   0 g
Carbohydrates   2g
Protein   0.2 g
Cholesterol   0 mg
Sodium   29 mg

Ingredients

2 C. seeded and coarsely chopped watermelon
2 tbsp chopped onion
3 tbsp seeded, chopped Anaheim chili
2 tbsp balsamic vinegar
1/4 tsp garlic salt

Directions

1. In a large bowl, mix together the watermelon, onion, chili pepper, balsamic vinegar and garlic salt.
2. Refrigerate, covered for at least 1 hour.

October's Melon Soup

Prep Time: 15 mins
Total Time: 2 hrs 15 mins

Servings per Recipe: 3
Calories   85 kcal
Fat   0.3 g
Carbohydrates   22g
Protein   1.3 g
Cholesterol   0 mg
Sodium   2 mg

Ingredients

4 C. cubed seeded watermelon
2 tbsp lemon juice
1 tbsp chopped fresh mint
1 tbsp honey

Directions

1. In a blender, add the watermelon, lemon juice, mint and honey and pulse till smooth.
2. Refrigerate for about 2 hours before serving.

JUBILANT
Juice

Prep Time: 5 mins
Total Time: 5 mins

Servings per Recipe: 4
Calories	35 kcal
Fat	0.1 g
Carbohydrates	8.9g
Protein	0.5 g
Cholesterol	0 mg
Sodium	4 mg

Ingredients

2 C. diced seedless watermelon
2 C. water
1 tbsp white sugar

Directions

1. In a blender, add the watermelon, water and sugar and pulse till smooth.

Picnic Salad

Prep Time: 20 mins
Total Time: 20 mins

Servings per Recipe: 4
Calories	35 kcal
Fat	0.1 g
Carbohydrates	8.9 g
Protein	0.5 g
Cholesterol	0 mg
Sodium	4 mg

Ingredients

2 small watermelons
1 (15 oz.) can canned diced pineapple in juice, drain juice and reserve
1 lb. seedless grapes
2 apples - peeled, cored and chopped
2 bananas, cut into bite-size pieces

Directions

1. Cut each watermelon in half lengthwise and with a melon baller, hollow out the insides, reserving rind for later use.
2. Drain the pineapple and discard the juice.
3. Cut apples in half, remove cores and cut into bite size pieces.
4. Peel the banana and slice in to bite size pieces.
5. Rinse the grapes under cold running water and pat dry.
6. In a bowl, toss together the watermelon balls, pineapple, apple, banana chunks, and grapes.
7. Divide fruit salad into the watermelon bowls and serve.

AQUA
Fresh

🍲 Prep Time: 10 mins
🕐 Total Time: 50 mins

Servings per Recipe: 6
Calories   177 kcal
Fat   0.6 g
Carbohydrates   45g
Protein   2.3 g
Cholesterol   0 mg
Sodium   7 mg

Ingredients

1/2 seedless watermelon
2 C. cold water
1/2 C. white sugar
1/2 C. water

Directions

1. Scoop the flesh from watermelon half.
2. In a blender, add the watermelon, 2 C. of the cold water and pulse till smooth.
3. Through a fine mesh strainer, strain into a large bowl and discard the fibers.
4. Skim and discard the excess foam from juice if desired.
5. In a pan, add the sugar and 1/2 C. of the water on medium heat and cook, stirring till the sugar is dissolved.
6. Remove from the heat and keep aside to cool in room temperature.
7. Add the sugar syrup in the bowl with the watermelon juice.
8. Transfer the mixture into a 2-quart pitcher and refrigerate for at least 30 minutes.
9. Fill the tall glasses with the ice cubes and pour agua fresca drink over the ice.
10. Serve with the straws.

New Age Pickles

Prep Time: 15 mins
Total Time: 21 hrs 15 mins

Servings per Recipe: 24
Calories   136 kcal
Fat   0.5 g
Carbohydrates   34.2g
Protein   0.7 g
Cholesterol   0 mg
Sodium   4624 mg

Ingredients

- 1 C. canning salt
- 1 gallon water
- 16 C. (1-inch) cubes watermelon rind
- 1 gallon water
- 3 cinnamon sticks
- 1 tsp whole allspice
- 1 tsp whole cloves
- 2 C. white vinegar (5% acidity)
- 3 C. white sugar
- 12 maraschino cherries, halved
- 1 lemon, thinly sliced
- 6 1-pint canning jars with lids and rings

Directions

1. In a large container, add the canning salt into 1 gallon water and stir till dissolved.
2. Stir in the watermelon rind.
3. With plastic wrap, cover the container and keep aside for about 12 hours.
4. Drain and rinse completely.
5. In a large pan, add the drained watermelon rind and 1 gallon water and bring to a boil.
6. Reduce the heat to medium-low and simmer for about 45-60 minutes.
7. Drain well and keep aside.
8. In a spice bag, place the cinnamon sticks, allspice and cloves.
9. In a pan, add the vinegar, sugar, spice bag, maraschino cherries and lemon slices and stir till the sugar is dissolved.
10. Add the watermelon rind and bring to a boil.
11. Reduce the heat to medium-low and simmer for about 5-10 minutes.
12. Remove the spice bag and keep aside.
13. Sterilize the jars and lids in boiling water for at least 5 minutes.
14. Put one whole clove into each jar.
15. Break cinnamon sticks into pieces and put 1 piece into each jar.

16. Place the watermelon rind with the vinegar mixture into the hot, sterilized jars, filling the within 1/4-inch of the top.
17. Run a knife round the insides of the jars to remove any air bubbles.
18. With a moist paper towel, wipe the rims of the jars to remove any food residue.
19. Top with the lids and screw on rings.
20. Place a rack in the bottom of a large pan and fill halfway with the water, then bring to a boil.
21. With a holder carefully, lower the jars into the boiling water, leaving a 2-inch space between the jars.
22. Bring the water to a rolling boil and process, covered about 10 minutes.
23. Remove the jars from the pan and place onto a wood surface, several inches apart to cool.
24. After cooling, press the top of each lid with a finger, ensuring that the seal is tight.
25. Store in a cool, dark area.

Simple Watermelon Salad

Prep Time: 20 mins
Total Time: 1 hr 20 mins

Servings per Recipe: 12
Calories	26 kcal
Fat	0.1 g
Carbohydrates	6.3g
Protein	0.5 g
Cholesterol	0 mg
Sodium	1 mg

Ingredients

6 C. cubed seeded watermelon
1/2 red onion, cut into thin half-moon slices
1/3 C. apple cider vinegar
2 tbsp chopped fresh mint
1/2 tsp ground black pepper

Directions

1. In a large bowl, add the watermelon, red onion, apple cider vinegar, mint and black pepper and toss to coat.
2. Refrigerate to chill for about 1 hour.

BEST
Pool-Side Treat

Prep Time: 10 mins
Total Time: 2 hrs 10 mins

Servings per Recipe: 6
Calories   174 kcal
Fat   0.3 g
Carbohydrates   21.1g
Protein   1.4 g
Cholesterol   0 mg
Sodium   4 mg

Ingredients

1 small watermelon, cut into 1-inch pieces
1 C. lemon lime soda

2 tbsp turbinado sugar

Directions

1. In a non-reactive container with a tight-fitting lid, add the watermelon.
2. Add the lemon lime soda and sugar and cover the container with the lid.
3. Shake the container till the watermelon the sugar is dissolved and watermelon is coated.
4. Refrigerate for about 2 hours to overnight.
5. Shake the mixture just before serving.

Watermelon Rind Lemongrass Jelly

Prep Time: 15 mins
Total Time: 1 hr 30 mins

Servings per Recipe: 20
Calories   32 kcal
Fat   0 g
Carbohydrates   8.1g
Protein   0 g
Cholesterol   0 mg
Sodium   175 mg

Ingredients

1/4 C. white sugar
1 C. diced watermelon rind, white parts only
1 1/2 tsp salt

1/2 C. water
1/2 C. white sugar
1 1/2 tsp lemon grass, chopped

Directions

1. Line a baking sheet with the parchment paper and sprinkle 1/4 C. of the sugar over the parchment evenly.
2. In a pan, add the watermelon rind and enough water to cover and bring to a boil.
3. Reduce the heat to medium and simmer for about 5 minutes.
4. Drain the watermelon rind and rinse the pan.
5. Return the watermelon to pan with the salt and enough water to cover the watermelon rind and bring to a boil.
6. Reduce the heat to medium and simmer for about 10 minutes.
7. Drain the watermelon rind and transfer into a bowl.
8. Rinse the pan.
9. In a the same pan, add 1/2 C. of the water, 1/2 C. of the white sugar and lemon grass and bring to a boil.
10. Add the watermelon rind and stir to coat.
11. Reduce the heat to medium-low and simmer for about 1 hour, stirring occasionally.
12. Transfer the watermelon rind to prepared baking sheet and roll to coat with sugar.
13. Store in an airtight container.

WATERMELON
Spritzer

Prep Time: 10 mins
Total Time: 10 mins

Servings per Recipe: 6
Calories	172 kcal
Fat	0.9 g
Carbohydrates	43.2g
Protein	3.5 g
Cholesterol	0 mg
Sodium	11 mg

Ingredients

6 slices watermelon, cubed
1 C. ice cubes
6 watermelon wedges
3 C. sparkling water

Directions

1. In a blender, add the watermelon and ice cubes and pulse till smooth.
2. Transfer the pureed watermelon into 6 cups and add enough sparkling water into each cup to fill to the top, then stir to combine.
3. Serve with a garnishing of the watermelon wedges.

Traditional Melon Dumplings

Prep Time: 15 mins
Total Time: 25 mins

Servings per Recipe: 12
Calories	320 kcal
Fat	2.8 g
Carbohydrates	73.7g
Protein	7.2 g
Cholesterol	2 mg
Sodium	308 mg

Ingredients

- 2 C. all-purpose flour
- 3/4 C. milk
- 4 tsp baking powder
- 1/2 tsp salt
- 1 tbsp vegetable shortening
- 1 C. water
- salt to taste
- 1 large watermelon, sliced into wedges

Directions

1. In a bowl, add the flour, milk, baking powder and 1/2 tsp of the salt and mix till a well combined dough is formed.
2. In a skillet, heat the shortening on medium heat.
3. Add the water and salt.
4. Form dough into 2x3/4-inch rectangles.
5. Place the dough rectangles in the skillet, leaving a small space between each.
6. Cover the skillet tightly and steam the dumplings for about 10-15 minutes.
7. Serve the dumplings with the sliced watermelon.

WATERMELON
Lunch Box Snack

Prep Time: 10 mins
Total Time: 10 mins

Servings per Recipe: 3
Calories	72 kcal
Fat	0.4 g
Carbohydrates	16.7g
Protein	1.8 g
Cholesterol	1 mg
Sodium	17 mg

Ingredients

2 1/2 C. cubed seeded watermelon
1 C. crushed ice
1/4 C. French vanilla yogurt

1 tbsp white sugar

Directions

1. In a blender, add the watermelon, ice, yogurt and sugar and pulse till smooth.

Winter Mint Cocktail

Prep Time: 10 mins
Total Time: 10 mins

Servings per Recipe: 10
Calories   164 kcal
Fat   0.3 g
Carbohydrates   21.9 g
Protein   1 g
Cholesterol   0 mg
Sodium   2 mg

Ingredients

10 C. diced seeded watermelon
1/2 C. water
1/3 C. agave nectar
1 1/2 C. tequila
1 C. frozen blueberries
1 sprig mint leaves, for garnish

Directions

1. In a blender, add the watermelon and pulse till smooth.
2. Transfer the juice into a large pitcher.
3. In a bowl, mix together the water and agave nectar.
4. Add the agave nectar mixture into the pitcher and stir to combine.
5. Add the tequila into the watermelon mixture and stir to combine.
6. Add the blueberries and serve with a garnishing of the mint.

3-INGREDIENT Smoothie

Prep Time: 5 mins
Total Time: 5 mins

Servings per Recipe: 2
Calories   109 kcal
Fat   0.2 g
Carbohydrates   28.8g
Protein   1 g
Cholesterol   0 mg
Sodium   4 mg

Ingredients

2 C. cubed seeded watermelon
5 ice cubes
2 tbsp honey

Directions

1. In a blender, add the watermelon, ice cubes and honey and pulse till smooth.

Cute Cookies

🥣 Prep Time: 20 mins
🕐 Total Time: 1 hr

Servings per Recipe: 18
Calories   223 kcal
Fat   10.5 g
Carbohydrates   31.1g
Protein   2 g
Cholesterol   19 mg
Sodium   134 mg

Ingredients

2 C. all-purpose flour
1 1/2 tsp baking powder
1/2 tsp salt
1/3 C. butter
1/2 C. shortening
3/4 C. white sugar
1 egg
1 tbsp milk

1 tsp vanilla extract
3 drops red food coloring
1/3 C. mini semi-sweet chocolate chips
1 1/2 C. confectioners' sugar
2 tbsp water
3 drops green food coloring

Directions

1. In a bowl, mix together the flour, baking powder and salt.
2. In another bowl, add the butter and shortening and with an electric mixer, beat at medium speed till fluffy.
3. Slowly, add the sugar, beating well.
4. Stir in the egg, milk and vanilla.
5. Slowly, add the flour mixture into the butter mixture, mixing well.
6. Add a small amount of the red food coloring to color dough as desired, beating till combined.
7. Shape the dough into a ball and refrigerate, covered to chill for at least 3 hours.
8. Set your oven to 375 degrees F.
9. Divide the dough in 2 portions.
10. Refrigerate 1 portion.
11. Place the remaining portion onto a lightly floured surface and roll into 1/4-inch thickness.
12. With a 3-inch round cookie cutter, cut the dough, then cut each circle in half.

13. Arrange the cookies onto an ungreased cookie sheet and press several chocolate chips in each cookie.
14. Repeat with the remaining dough.
15. Cook in the oven for about 8-10 minutes.
16. Cool on wire racks.
17. For frosting in a bowl, add the powdered sugar and water and mix till smooth.
18. Add a small amount of green food coloring, mixing till combined.
19. Dip round edge of each cookie in green frosting and arrange onto a wax paper till frosting is firm.

East Latin Chili Lime Melon Snack

Prep Time: 10 mins
Total Time: 10 mins

Servings per Recipe: 2
Calories   51 kcal
Fat   0.4 g
Carbohydrates   12.8g
Protein   1.1 g
Cholesterol   0 mg
Sodium   296 mg

Ingredients

- 1/4 tsp ground cumin
- 1/4 tsp ground coriander
- 1/4 tsp chili powder
- 1/4 tsp salt
- 1/8 tsp cayenne pepper
- 2 C. cubed seeded watermelon
- 1/2 lime, juiced

Directions

1. In a bowl, mix together the cumin, coriander, chili powder, salt and cayenne pepper.
2. In a serving bowl, place the watermelon.
3. Sprinkle with the spice mixture and drizzle with the lime juice.

SIMPLY
Watermelon

Prep Time: 15 mins
Total Time: 15 mins

Servings per Recipe: 8
Calories   51 kcal
Fat   0.3 g
Carbohydrates   12.9g
Protein   1 g
Cholesterol   0 mg
Sodium   2 mg

Ingredients

1 small watermelon, seeded and cubed

Directions

1. In a blender, add the watermelon and pulse till smooth.

Melon Jell-O Pie

Prep Time: 10 mins
Total Time: 3 hrs 10 mins

Servings per Recipe: 8
Calories	332 kcal
Fat	18.1 g
Carbohydrates	41.3g
Protein	3 g
Cholesterol	0 mg
Sodium	206 mg

Ingredients

1 (3 oz.) package watermelon flavored Jell-O(R)
1/4 C. water
1 (12 oz.) container frozen whipped topping, thawed
2 C. watermelon
1 (9 inch) prepared graham cracker crust

Directions

1. In a bowl, mix together the watermelon gelatin and water.
2. Fold the gelatin mixture into the dessert topping.
3. Stir in the cut watermelon.
4. Place mixture into graham cracker crust and refrigerate to chill for about 3 hours.

SUGAR FREE
Cocktail

Prep Time: 5 mins
Total Time: 5 mins

Servings per Recipe: 1
Calories	82 kcal
Fat	0.6 g
Carbohydrates	20.1g
Protein	2.4 g
Cholesterol	0 mg
Sodium	255 mg

Ingredients

1 C. coconut water
1/2 C. watermelon puree
1 tsp stevia

1/2 C. ice cubes

Directions

1. In a blender, add the coconut water, watermelon and stevia and pulse till smooth.
2. Fill a cocktail shaker with the ice and add the watermelon mixture.
3. Cover shaker and shake till chilled.
4. Transfer into a glass.

Maine Inspired Lemonade

Prep Time: 10 mins
Total Time: 15 mins

Servings per Recipe: 12
Calories   50 kcal
Fat   0.1 g
Carbohydrates   13g
Protein   0.3 g
Cholesterol   0 mg
Sodium   6 mg

Ingredients

1/2 C. white sugar
1/2 C. water
4 C. cubed watermelon
3 C. cold water
1/2 C. fresh lemon juice

6 C. ice cubes

Directions

1. In a blender, add the watermelon and pulse till smooth.
2. Through a fine mesh sieve, strain the pureed watermelon.
3. In a pan, add the sugar and 1/2 C. of the water and bring to a boil on medium-high heat.
4. Cook for about 5 minutes, stirring continuously.
5. Remove from the heat and stir in 3 C. of the cold water and lemon juice.
6. Divide the ice into 12 glasses and top with 2-3 tbsp of the pureed watermelon and lemonade.
7. Gently stir before serving.

RED WHITE
and Preserves

Prep Time: 15 mins
Total Time: 2 hrs 25 mins

Servings per Recipe: 40
Calories   66 kcal
Fat   0.1 g
Carbohydrates   17.6 g
Protein   0.2 g
Cholesterol   0 mg
Sodium   1 mg

Ingredients

2 lb. watermelon
3 C. white sugar
3 lemons - rinsed, sliced and seeded

Directions

1. Remove the green rind of the melon and chop the white part into small cubes, leaving the red flesh mostly intact.
2. Discard the seeds.
3. In a heavy pan, add 4 C. of the prepared watermelon, sugar and lemons on medium heat and bring to a boil.
4. Boil slowly for about 2 hours, stirring occasionally.
5. Sterilize the jars and lids in boiling water for at least 5 minutes.
6. Place the jam into the hot, sterilized jars, filling the jars to within 1/4-inch of the top.
7. Run a knife around the insides of the jars to remove any air bubbles.
8. With a moist paper towel, wipe the rims of the jars to remove any food residue.
9. Top with the lids and screw on rings.
10. Place a rack in the bottom of a large pan and fill halfway with the water.
11. Bring to a boil on high heat.
12. With a holder, carefully lower the jars into the pan, leaving a 2-inch space between the jars.
13. Bring the water to a full boil and process, covered for about 10 minutes.

Puppy Dog Slush Pops

Prep Time: 35 mins
Total Time: 3 hrs 35 mins

Servings per Recipe: 16
Calories   134 kcal
Fat   3.6 g
Carbohydrates   24.7 g
Protein   1.5 g
Cholesterol   8 mg
Sodium   76 mg

Ingredients

1 C. sugar
1 (3 oz.) package JELL-O Lime Flavor Gelatin
2 C. boiling water, divided
Ice cubes
1 C. cold water, divided
1 (3 oz.) package JELL-O Strawberry Flavor Gelatin
3 tbsp miniature semi-sweet chocolate chips
4 oz. PHILADELPHIA Cream Cheese, softened
1 1/2 C. thawed COOL WHIP Whipped Topping

Directions

1. In a bowl, mix together 1/3 C. of the sugar and lime gelatin mix.
2. Add 1 C. of the boiling water and stir till dissolved completely.
3. Add enough ice into 1/2 C. cold water to measure about 3/4 C.
4. Add into the bowl with the lime gelatin and stir till the ice melts completely.
5. Refrigerate for about 25 minutes.
6. Meanwhile, repeat Step 1 using strawberry gelatin mix and omit the refrigeration step.
7. In 16 (3-oz.) paper cups, divide the strawberry gelatin mixture and freeze for about 20 minutes.
8. Add 1/2 tsp of the chocolate chips in each cup and stir to combine.
9. In a bowl, add the cream cheese and remaining sugar and beat till well combined.
10. Stir in the COOL WHIP.
11. Spread the cream cheese mixture over the gelatin in cups.
12. Place the lime gelatin over the cream cheese mixture evenly.
13. Insert the wooden pop stick in center of each cup and freeze for at least 3 hours.
14. Remove the pops from cups just before serving.

COUNTRY
Smoothie

Prep Time: 10 mins
Total Time: 10 mins

Servings per Recipe: 4
Calories	94 kcal
Fat	2.8 g
Carbohydrates	12.9 g
Protein	4.9 g
Cholesterol	11 mg
Sodium	57 mg

Ingredients

1 1/2 C. diced watermelon
2 1/4 C. milk
2 tsp white sugar

Directions

1. In a blender, add the watermelon and milk and pulse till smooth.
2. Add the sugar and pulse for about 10 seconds more.
3. Serve immediately.

Fruit Gazpacho

Prep Time: 10 mins
Total Time: 30 mins

Servings per Recipe: 6
Calories	110 kcal
Fat	4.8 g
Carbohydrates	16.4g
Protein	1.8 g
Cholesterol	0 mg
Sodium	3 mg

Ingredients

- 2 C. 1/4-inch-diced watermelon
- 2 C. orange juice
- 2 tbsp extra-virgin olive oil
- 1 seedless cucumber, cut into 1/4-inch dice
- 1 small yellow bell pepper, seeded and cut into 1/4-inch dice
- 1 small onion, cut into 1/4-inch dice
- 2 medium garlic cloves, minced
- 1 small jalapeno pepper, seeded and minced (optional)
- 3 tbsp fresh lime juice
- 2 tbsp chopped fresh parsley
- Salt and freshly ground black pepper

Directions

1. In a blender, add 1/2 C. of the watermelon, orange juice and oil and pulse till smooth.
2. Transfer the mixture into a bowl with the remaining ingredients and stir to combine.
3. Refrigerate before serving.

AUGUST'S Orange Vanilla Smoothie

Prep Time: 5 mins
Total Time: 5 mins

Servings per Recipe: 1
Calories   494 kcal
Fat   23.7 g
Carbohydrates   69.3g
Protein   7.5 g
Cholesterol   85 mg
Sodium   75 mg

Ingredients

1 1/2 C. frozen strawberries
1 1/2 C. frozen diced watermelon
1/4 C. cream
1/4 C. plain yogurt
2 tbsp orange juice

1 tbsp white sugar (optional)
1/4 tsp vanilla extract

Directions

1. In a blender, add the strawberries, watermelon, cream, yogurt, orange juice, sugar and vanilla and pulse till smooth.

Mexican Melon Juice

Prep Time: 25 mins
Total Time: 25 mins

Servings per Recipe: 8
Calories   72 kcal
Fat   0.1 g
Carbohydrates   18.7g
Protein   0.5 g
Cholesterol   0 mg
Sodium   2 mg

Ingredients

4 C. cubed seeded watermelon
1/2 C. water
1/2 C. white sugar
4 slices lime

24 fresh mint leaves
ice

Directions

1. In a blender, add the watermelon and sugar and pulse till smooth.
2. Cut the lime slices in half and place a half lime slice in each glass with 3 mint leaves.
3. With a cocktail muddler, crush the lime and mint leaves.
4. Fill each glass with the ice and place the watermelon on top.
5. Stir before serving.

SOUTHERN Rosemary Lemonade

Prep Time: 15 mins
Total Time: 1 hr 15 mins

Servings per Recipe: 8
Calories   156 kcal
Fat   0.3 g
Carbohydrates   41.2g
Protein   1.6 g
Cholesterol   0 mg
Sodium   12 mg

Ingredients

2 C. water
3/4 C. white sugar
1 sprig rosemary, leaves stripped and chopped
2 C. lemon juice

12 C. cubed seeded watermelon
8 C. ice cubes

Directions

1. In a small pan, add the water and sugar and bring to a boil on high heat.
2. Stir in the rosemary and keep aside to steep for about 1 hour.
3. Through a mesh strainer, strain the rosemary syrup in a blender.
4. Add half of the lemon juice and half of the watermelon and pulse till smooth.
5. Strain the mixture into a pitcher.
6. Now, add the remaining lemon juice and watermelon in the blender and pulse till smooth.
7. Transfer the watermelon mixture into the pitcher and stir to combine.
8. Serve in glasses over the ice.

Fiesta Candy

Prep Time: 1 hr
Total Time: 10 d 1 h 15 m

Servings per Recipe: 8
Calories   156 kcal
Fat   0.3 g
Carbohydrates   41.2g
Protein   1.6 g
Cholesterol   0 mg
Sodium   12 mg

Ingredients

2 1/2 gallons water
1 tbsp salt
2 gallons watermelon rind, white part only, cut into 1-inch cubes
1 quart cider vinegar
26 C. white sugar, divided
28 whole cloves
14 (3 inch) cinnamon stick

Directions

1. In a large pan, add the water and salt and bring to a boil on high heat.
2. Add the watermelon rinds and bring to a boil.
3. Cook for about 20 minutes.
4. Drain the rinds in a colander.
5. In a pan, add the vinegar and 6 C. of the sugar and bring to a boil.
6. Remove from the heat and stir in the watermelon rinds.
7. Immediately, cover the pan and keep aside for overnight.
8. The following day, with a slotted spoon, remove the rinds from the syrup and transfer them into a clean bowl.
9. Place the pan of syrup on high heat.
10. Add 4 C. of the sugar and bring to a boil.
11. Boil till the sugar is dissolved.
12. Remove from the heat and stir in the watermelon rinds.
13. Immediately, cover the pan and keep aside for overnight.
14. On 3rd day, with a slotted spoon, remove the rinds from the syrup and transfer them into a clean bowl.
15. Place the pan of syrup on high heat.
16. Add 2 C. of the sugar and bring to a boil.
17. Boil till the sugar is dissolved.

18. Remove from the heat and stir in the watermelon rinds.
19. Immediately, cover the pan and keep aside for overnight.
20. Repeat the step 3 every day for 6 more days.
21. On day 10, in boiling water, sterilize the canning jars, rings and lids.
22. Place the watermelon rinds into sterilized jars, making sure there are no spaces or air pockets on the sides.
23. Add 2 cloves and 1 cinnamon stick in each jar.
24. Return the syrup to a boil and pour over watermelon rind in each jar, within 1/4-inch of the top.
25. Top with lids and screw on rings.
26. Place a rack in the bottom of a large pan and fill halfway with the boiling water.
27. With a holder, carefully lower the jars in the pan, leaving a 2-inch space between jars.
28. Bring the water to a full boil and process, covered for about 10-15 minutes.
29. Remove the pan from the heat and keep the jars stand in the water for about 2 hours.
30. Remove the jars from the pan and place onto a cloth-covered surface, several inches apart to cool completely.
31. After cooling, press the top of each lid with a finger, ensuring that the seal is tight.
32. Preserve in a cool, dark place for 2 weeks before opening.

Party Punch

Prep Time: 45 mins
Total Time: 45 mins

Servings per Recipe: 8
Calories	156 kcal
Fat	0.3 g
Carbohydrates	41.2g
Protein	1.6 g
Cholesterol	0 mg
Sodium	12 mg

Ingredients

- 1 1/2 C. fresh raspberries
- 3 sprigs fresh mint leaves
- 1 seeded, cubed watermelon
- 1 C. strawberry margarita mix
- 1 C. coconut-flavored rum
- 2 C. ice cubes
- 8 mint sprigs to garnish

Directions

1. In a blender, add the raspberries and mint leaves and pulse till smooth.
2. Strain the mixture into a serving pitcher.
3. Now, add the cubed watermelon in the blender and pulse till smooth.
4. Strain the watermelon juice into the pitcher with the raspberry mixture.
5. Add the margarita mix, coconut rum and ice cubes and stir to combine.
6. Serve with a garnishing of the mint sprigs.

MELON and Cheese Snacks

Prep Time: 15 mins
Total Time: 15 mins

Servings per Recipe: 1
Calories   45 kcal
Fat   3 g
Carbohydrates   2.7g
Protein   2.2 g
Cholesterol   12 mg
Sodium   157 mg

Ingredients

8 (1 inch) cubes watermelon
8 (1/2 inch) cubes feta cheese
8 fresh mint leaves

8 bamboo toothpicks

Directions

1. Thread 1 watermelon cube, 1 feta cheese cube and 1 mint leaf onto each toothpick and serve.

Honey Popsicles

Prep Time: 10 mins
Total Time: 2 hrs 10 mins

Servings per Recipe: 6
Calories	31 kcal
Fat	0.1 g
Carbohydrates	8.1g
Protein	0.3 g
Cholesterol	0 mg
Sodium	1 mg

Ingredients

- 1 1/2 C. watermelon, seeded and diced
- 1/2 C. water
- 1 tbsp honey
- 1 tbsp fresh lemon juice
- 1 tbsp white sugar

Directions

1. In a blender, add the watermelon, water, honey, lemon juice and sugar and pulse till smooth.
2. Divide the mixture into ice pop molds and freeze for about 2 hours.
3. Run hot water over ice pop molds for a few seconds to unmold.

SUMMER Fruit Salad

Prep Time: 15 mins
Total Time: 1 hr 15 mins

Servings per Recipe: 4
Calories	162 kcal
Fat	1.2 g
Carbohydrates	40.9 g
Protein	2.1 g
Cholesterol	0 mg
Sodium	5 mg

Ingredients

- 4 C. coarsely chopped seedless watermelon
- 4 C. seedless red grapes, halved
- 2 tbsp grated lemon zest
- 2 tbsp grated lime zest

Directions

1. In a bowl, mix together the watermelon, red grapes, lemon zest and lime zest and gently toss to coat.
2. Refrigerate, covered for about 1 hour

Persian
Melon Salad

Prep Time: 30 mins
Total Time: 1 hr 30 mins

Servings per Recipe: 12
Calories   194 kcal
Carbohydrates   48.8 g
Cholesterol   0 mg
Fat   0.9 g
Protein   2.8 g
Sodium   47 mg

Ingredients

- one honeydew melon, fruit removed with a melon baller
- one cantaloupe, fruit removed with a melon baller
- 1/4 watermelon, fruit removed with a melon baller
- one bunch grapes
- one pineapple - peeled, cored, and cut into chunks
- 2 tbsps pickled ginger
- one cup fresh orange juice
- 1/4 cup fresh lime juice
- one tbsp white sugar
- 1/4 cup chopped fresh mint
- one pint fresh strawberries, hulled (optional)
- 4 sprigs fresh mint for garnish

Directions

1. Get a bowl mix the following: chopped mint, honeydew, sugar, watermelon, lime juice, grapes, orange juice, pineapple, and pickled ginger.
2. Cover the bowl refrigerate for one hour.
3. Add strawberries and mint.
4. Enjoy.

ENJOY THE RECIPES?

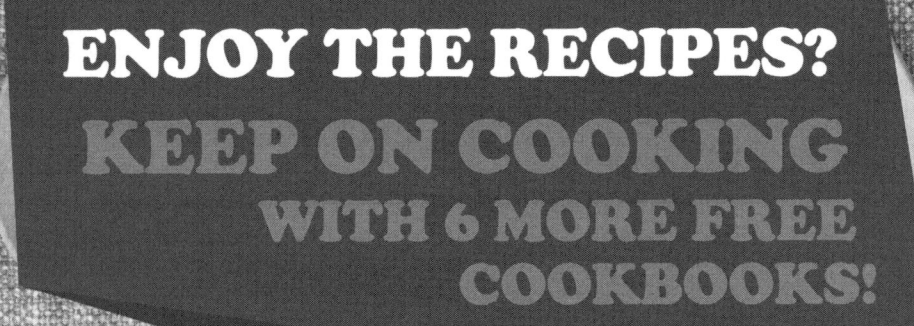

KEEP ON COOKING WITH 6 MORE FREE COOKBOOKS!

Visit our website and simply enter your email address to join the club and receive your 6 cookbooks.

http://booksumo.com/magnet

https://www.instagram.com/booksumopress/

https://www.facebook.com/booksumo/

Printed in Great Britain
by Amazon